FORMULATION
IN
PSYCHOTHERAPY

CONNOR WHITELEY

ACKNOWLEDGMENTS
Thank you to you all my wonderful readers without them I couldn't do what I love.

PART ONE: INTRODUCTION TO FORMULATION

INTRODUCTION

As always I hate long boring introductions, so I'll keep this short.

As you'll learn throughout this book, formulation is a critical skill in clinical psychology and I love it.

Why Read This Book?

If you want to become a clinical psychologist or you're interested in becoming a therapist then formulation is a needed skill that you will have to learn.

So, this book gives you a great look at all the different topics within formulation to give you a great overview and a basic understanding. That should put you ahead of your peers.

In this book, you'll learn about the different approaches to formulation. Like:

- Case Formulation in CBT
- Psychodynamic Approach
- Systemic Approach
- Integrative Approach

- Team Formulations
- Controversies and Debates about Formulation
- And more…

What I love about this book is that you get to learn about a lot of great information and it's all explained in an easy to understand way!

Who Is This Book For?

Regardless of whether you're a student or a trained professional you should find this book useful as well as interesting.

If you're a student, then this book will give you a great overview of the amazing topic of formulation. Looking at the many different approaches to formulation that you can take in the future.

If you're a trained psychology professional, then this book should be useful as it reminds you of previous training and it will introduce you to other approaches. That you might want to be trained in later on.

Equally, it may introduce you to new ways of working that can benefit your clients.

Who Am I?

In case you're like me, I always like to know who the author is when I read a nonfiction book.

Therefore, I am Connor Whiteley, a University Psychology student at the University of Kent, England. I am the author of over 10 psychology books, I run a weekly blog at connorwhiteley.net and I'm the host of the weekly The Psychology World Podcast. Available on all major podcasting apps.

Finally, I'm writing this book because I love the topic of formulation and I want to share this amazing topic with you.

So, please join to find out what formulation is and the different ways to do it!

CHAPTER 1: WHAT IS FORMULATION

At last, I'm doing an entire book dedicated to formulation. This book I'm very excited about because I have always loved the idea of formulation in psychology as well as psychotherapy.

And this book allowed me to explore my interest in a much greater depth.

However, this raises the massive question of: what is formulation in psychology?

If you've read my Clinical Psychology book then you may already have some idea but this book will built upon this information in a LOT more depth.

So, regardless of whether you have never heard of formulation before, only have a small amount of knowledge about it (like me before writing this book) or you know a lot about formulation. Hopefully, you will get something out of this book.

What is Formulation?

In essence, formulation can be understood as a hypothesis to be tested because Butler (1998) states that formulation is 'the tool used by clinicians to relate theory to practice'

Nonetheless, that isn't the only definition of formulation due to other notable figures in Clinical Psychology have made their own definitions as well.

- "A psychotherapy case formulation is essentially a hypothesis about the causes, precipitants and maintaining influences of a persons psychological, interpersonal and behavioural problems" (Eells, 1997, p.4).
- "A process of ongoing collaborative sense-making" (Harper and Moss, 2003, p. 8).

I must mention that in the topic of Formulation there is one very important figure called: Lucy Johnstone and she is a massive figure and a great author on the topic of formulation.

Therefore, her definition needs to be highlighted:

"Formulation can be defined as the process of co-constructing a hypothesis or 'best guess' about the origins of a person's difficulties in the context of their relationships, social circumstances, life events, and the sense that they have made of them. It provides a structure for thinking together with the client or service user about how to understand their experiences and how to move forward. Formulation draws on two equally important sources of evidence: the clinician brings knowledge derived from theory, research, and clinical experience, while the service user brings expertise about their own life and the meaning and impact of their relationships and circumstances". (Johnstone, 2018)

I mean you cannot get a better as well as more comprehensive definition as the one above.

However, in case you're like me and you tend to skip massive complex paragraphs. I've given you a summarised version below.

In short, when a formulation is broken down it summarises the client's core problems and it shows how the client's difficulties are related to one another.

In addition, it uses psychological theory to explain why and how the client's difficulties are happening to help plan an intervention.

Why is Formulation Important to Know About?

In all honesty, if formulation wasn't important to be aware of then I'm afraid that I wouldn't have looked into it.

Simply, because I love psychology, like you, but there are simply too many areas to investigate.

Therefore, if you intend to go into clinical psychology as a profession, you need to know about Formulation as this is a major topic, and it's very important for various reasons. This you'll discover throughout the later chapters.

Another reason formulation is important is because it's considered a skill by the Health and Care Professionals Council, as well as according to the Division of Clinical Psychology (2010) formulation can be the defining competency of the profession.

In other words, if you want to do clinical psychology as a job then you NEED to know about formulation.

If you want to know more information about the subfield then please check out Clinical Psychology for more information.

Building Upon this Further:

In formulation, there are a lot of different approaches that can be taken to create a formulation. Like: negative thoughts in CBT, narrative therapy and psychodynamic. Over the course of the book, we'll look at roughly 6 approaches.

In addition, a formulation applies the theory to an individual and their own unique difficulties.

Interestingly, the term formulation can be used as an event and a process. You'll see this in more detail in later chapters but you can give a formulation (event) to someone and you can create a formulation with the client. (process)

Another example is most definitions like the ones above are formed as if formulation are only concrete events. Like: a letter to written assignment and so on.

However, as you'll see later, this is not always the case.

Personally, I prefer to think about formulations as a creative process because ideally you should be working with the client to create a formulation that best fits them.

Equally, I do understand why formulations are sometimes events.

Anyway, you'll see this in more detail when we get into the meat of the book.

Basic Make Up of a Formulation:

In a formulation, there are a range of common elements regardless of the therapeutic model used. For example, each type of formulation makes a hypothesis about a person's difficulties which draws upon psychological theory.

In addition, all formulations summarise the client's core problems by drawing on psychological principles and theory that allow you to see how a client's problems are related.

Additionally, they allow the therapist to suggest why these difficulties have developed at this time in this situation.

Finally, all formulations are open to revision or reformulating because they need to be 'accurate' and 'corrected' if something is 'wrong' in the formulation.

With the entire point being the formulation is used to plan or guide an intervention for the client to help them live a better, happier life.

On the other hand, formulation is different from the traditional therapeutic models. In terms of:

- The most important factors
- Emphasis on reflectivity
- Explanatory concepts they draw on.
- Emphasis on expert vs collaborative stance
- And more

Although, a formulation could be described as a double-edged sword as the formulation could reveal no intervention is needed. Or the formulation itself could be therapeutic as it gives the client a greater understanding of their difficulties.

(I thought I would include that piece of debate about formulation to start you thinking critically about formulation. But we have an entire section dedicated to the debates about formulation. So, personally, I would focus on enjoying the book and think critically later)

Additional Purposes of Formulation:

In addition, to the other purposes we've discussed in this chapter, according to DCP (2011:8) formulation could serve other purposes as well. For example:

- Ensuring a cultural understanding has been incorporated into the intervention.
- Strengthening the therapeutic alliance.
- Helping the client to feel understood.
- Normalising the client's difficulties.
- Increasing sense of agency, hope and meaning.
- And more.

Benefits of Team Formulation:

There is a later chapter dedicated to team formulation but I love the topic, so I wanted to add that another benefit of formulation is teamwork. Due to formulation provides a team with a consistent approach to intervention. Which draws on the expertise of all team members.

And most importantly, it minimises blame as well as disagreement in the team. Whilst, raising morale and facilitating culture change (DCP, 2011;9) in the process.

Who knew one 'simple' task could accomplish so much!

Best practices:

Moving onto the last section of our introductory chapter, like any therapist technique, formulation can be harmful as well as be helpful, of course, depending on how a clinician uses it.

Therefore, this was addressed in the DCP guidelines (2011) which includes an event and process checklist which when combined with Buter (1998) means a formulation needs to meet the following criteria:

- It needs to be grounded in an appropriate depth and level of breath.
- Culturally sensitive.
- Use accessible language so anyone can understand the formulation.
- Consider the possible role of trauma and abuse.
- Possible that the service could be confounding the problem.
- Informed by social/ societal and service/ organisational factors and more.

We'll explore these more throughout the book.

Subsequently, the checklist for best practices for formulation as a process are:

- Be clear about who the formulation is for.
- Who has the problem?
- Construct formulation collaboratively.
- Provide a rationale for choices.
- Reflective about their own assumption and values.

So now that you've learnt what formulation is, how is formulation used in Cognitive Behavioural Therapy?

CHAPTER 2: CASE FORMULATION IN CBT

Personally, I think Cognitive Behavioural Therapy or CBT has to be one of the best well-known therapeutic approaches. Probably, because it's used in the treatment of depression which is fairly common.

As a short introduction, CBT is a type of psychotherapy based on Aron Beck's Theory of Depression. The theory proposes that cognition is the main reason behind depression and focuses on the impact that a change in automatic thoughts can have on behaviour. The theory focuses on:

- The cognitive triad- negative beliefs about the self, the world and the future. These influence the automatic thoughts to be pessimistic.
- Negative schema- the negative beliefs about themselves become generalize and people start to think negatively about everything that happens to them.

- Faulty thinking patterns- people think and make illogical conclusions because of how they process information is biased.

If you want to learn more about depression and CBT then please check out Abnormal Psychology 2nd Edition and Clinical Psychology.

Formulation in CBT:

Moving into our main topic, formulation is critical in CBT because Bulter (1998) thought case formulation can be described as the 'lynchpin' of CBT.

The main reason being creating a formulation for each case can lead to an improvement in practice.

As a result, the formulation can explain the client's representations (also known as what symptoms or difficulties they are showing) in a theoretical coherent and meaningful way which can lead to more effective interventions.

In essence, it allows the client's experience and the theory, skills, and knowledge that therapists bring to be combined to produce a formulation.

Ultimately, this information makes it understandable why formulation is a key concept in CBT. (Beck, 2011)

Furthermore, CBT case formulation is widely used in clinical practice because the formulation is principles-based than a specific template or manual.

In Cognitive Behavioural Therapy, the three principles are:

- Process of change (heal)
- Which develops over time.
- The end result is made up of several ingredients. Such as: protective and risk factors, theory, experiences and so on.

Nonetheless, the principles don't exist alone as the 5ps are critical in CBT so a therapist can understand the wide range of factors that interact to produce the client's representations.

The 5P Model:

The 5P model provides a structure to a formulation and as long as you stick to the language being used by the formulation you can use the 5P model in a number of different models.

The 5P model is:

- Predisposing- factors that make the individual vulnerable to a disorder.
- Precipitating- factors that trigger the problem.
- Presenting- this refers to both the what the individual is reporting and what other people are reporting as a problem.

- perpetuation- factors; like: mechanisms; that keep a problem going or unintended side-effects of coping strategies.
- Protective- factors that will help the resistance and indicate the person has other strengths or interests that they can use to overcome the problem.

Each of these factors are very important in Clinical practice as you need to know each of these 5Ps in order to fully understand what's happening to your client, and it's this full understanding that will allow you to help the patient better.

Ultimately, allowing flexibility and the formulation can be tailored to client, not vice versa.

Personally, I love CBT case formulation because you can have a lot of fun with it. As you can use lots of different types of worksheets to help you and your client. Plus, you can get very visual with CBT.

Collaborative empiricism:

Thankfully, in my opinion, CBT is an approach to therapy and formulation that places a high emphasis on collaboration with the client. This is good as it makes the client feel valued and empowered.

In addition, in terms of formulation, it means the therapist and the client can work together to make the best formulation they can. Meaning that the therapist can plan an intervention that best matches their client.

Also, CBT's emphasis on the current problem instead of childhood memories and the like make it good for people who want to focus on the now.

Co-Morbidity:

Although, within the Cognitive Behavioural approach, there is a possible problem because due to co-morbidity and the fact that most CBT research is done with only one disorder. There isn't a manual or a lot of training, if any, about how to use CBT when you're treating two disorders. For example, depression and a personality disorder.

Meaning that there's a lot of art in its application.

Key characteristics of CBT formulation:

As a quick summary, case formulation in CBT is based on the cognitive model and it utilises many core concepts. Such as: schemas, conditional assumptions and rules.

Additionally, the formulation is developed in levels from presenting to predisposition. (The 5P model) as well as there is a strong emphasis on being evidence based with a collaborative or co-creation stance on making the formulation.

Earlier I mentioned childhood memories, so how does formulation work using the psychodynamic model?

PART TWO: PSYCHODYMANIC FORMULATION

CHAPTER 3: PSYCHODYAMNIC FORMULATION

Personally, I think psychodynamic is a very interesting approach. Simply because of the public's perception and even within the psychology community there is still a lot of dislike for it.

Although, this is still a very well used approach in psychology and as I disgust in my Clinical Psychology book. Freud's ideas are very influential and shouldn't be disregarded as crazy talk.

Psychodynamic Approach:

You're probably quite familiar with the Psychodynamic Approach but if you aren't then you can read about it in my FREE eBook: What is Psychology?

Although, there will be a brief explanation throughout this section.

So, in the Psychodynamic Approach, there is no one

psychodynamic theory and no single psychodynamic formulation.

As a result, there are many different psychodynamic theories with competing visions, assumptions and possible conceptualisations. All leading to endless debating.

Although, in modern times, the psychodynamic approach is used generally for all approaches connected to the psychanalytic roots.

Interestingly, the use of formulation is related to its confused complexities. It's this unknown that's useful and a value as well as a hold key in modern psychodynamic. As when dealing with the cognitive unconscious it's impossible not to presumable you know too much.

Overall, formulation is not a secure guide to the human psyche and each theory has its own formulation. But all psychodynamic formulation has the unknown as a commonality. (Leiper and Maltly, 2004)

Due to, the entire basis of the psychodynamic approach is discovering the unconscious content of the human psyche.

Saying that, therapists aren't focused on the unity of ideas that Freud believed critical to protect the analytic ideal. (The Id, Ego and Superego)

Instead, it's the key perspective and values of the human condition; rather than conceptualisation; and it could be considered pre-theoretical. This shared vision amongst the psychodynamic approach forms a great basis for formulation.

Due to instead of looking at a person through a psychological paradigm. They look through the idea of sensibility about the nature of therapeutic practice.

In other words, the therapist is looking at the client collaboratively and this is great as it allows diversity of ideas, as well as it provides us an idea about what an accurate and useful formulation could look like.

Core Features in Psychodynamic Formulation:

Like other approaches, psychodynamic has its own core features that makes it very different from other approaches in psychology and psychotherapy.

For instance, the psychodynamic approach to formulation focuses on the emotional or psychodynamic pain of the client, and the psyche construction in the struggle of life, the client's difficulties, to deal with them.

In other words, the approach looks at the make-up or how the client's psyche is constructed so we can find how the client's 'defence mechanisms' deal with the client's difficulties.

Furthermore, there's a core feature called 'dynamics' this is the turbulence creation in this struggle and currents of mental life- as well as the psychodynamic approach looks at the methods of avoiding this pain of the client develops. Due to we use certain ways of thinking, seeing, behaving and more to make sense of these methods and their purpose.

Overall, most of the psychodynamic approach to formulation focuses on the unconscious as the Unconscious influences the way we live our lives.

How Does the Unconscious Cause Mental Distress?

According to psychodynamic theory, our unconscious attempts to help us avoid psychological pain, but often these attempts fail.

Although, we keep repeating these failed attempts at avoiding the pain and this maintains the mental condition.

Resulting, in therapy being important because the therapy allows the client to get in touch with ourselves, as well as the unconscious content that is hidden from our conscious mind.

Ultimately, therapy is about helping the client to reformulate their experiences in more inclusive ways. As well as it expands the client's awareness and this opens up new ways of managing their struggles.

CHAPTER 4: THE PSYCHODYNMIC PERSPECTIVE

I promise you in a minute, we will get into the verbal meat of psychodynamic formulation but I need to quickly mention that a vital implication of Freud's theory is that all actions can be understood through the logic of the unconscious.

Therefore, if you cannot understand why someone does something then try to think about the behaviour in terms of the Id, Ego and Superego.

I know that it sounds bizarre but… you never know.

Dynamic Perspective:

Moving onto the topic at hand, we're now going to look at formulation in the psychodynamic approach and as I mentioned earlier there are different theories and perspectives to take in psychodynamic formulations. Hence, the different sections coming up.

Firstly, the Dynamic Perspective is the process of constructing or discovering meaning in the client's unclear as well as confusing psyche or unconscious. Here, the aim of the formulation is to retell the story as intentional and meaningful.

Meaning, instead of the client's psyche being confused and chaotic. You try to make sense of the 'chaos' and retell the content as a coherent and intentional story.

Additionally, the dynamic perspective views mental life as a constant flow influenced by interacting forces.

In much simpler terms, this perspective sees the unconscious as wishing to avoid emotional pain by concealing its source. Which, according to the psychodynamic approach, is caused by an inner conflict between ourselves. Like: the Id, Ego and Superego.

To summarise the dynamic perspective, personal difficulties are considered in terms of the client's meaning and motivation.

Therefore, formulations are conflicted desires as well as relationships that generate unmanageable anxiety.

Following this, the client's psychological defences surface with our presenting symptoms to protect is from overwhelming anxiety.

For example, a person with social anxiety shows the symptom of avoiding or being fearful of social groups to protect them from previous emotional trauma.

As a result, a psychodynamic formulation must include:

- What's the main underlying conflict?
- What are the self-other relationship impulses as well as fears that make up these conflicts?
- What defensive strategies and relationship patterns are delayed to manage these anxieties?
- How effective are they are at dealing with their maladaptive impacts?
- How are the presenting symptoms or problems related to these underlying conflicts and defensive strategies?

Structural Perspective:

Following on from our last psychodynamic perspective, the structural perspective focuses on the mental framework of the client's psychological functioning and the differences in psychological structures people have.

One way, this perspective does this is it focuses on the different levels of organisation in the client's mind. For instance, the differences in how the unconscious and conscious realm function.

Due to the conscious is structured by verbal syntax, for example.

Whereas the unconscious realm isn't ordered and there's no sense of time.

Why is the Structural Perspective Important?

In psychodynamic theory, the internal world is dominant, and this makes our perception of the world and our experiences conform to our internal world.

Resulting in the Structural perspective looking at the relationship between our internal and external realities to see if our perception is reality based or made up of distorted internal perceptions.

You only need to think of Beck (1967) and the faulty thinking patterns as well as the negative cognitive style (Alloy, Abramson and Francis, 1999) of Depressed People to see the logic behind this perspective.

To summarise, the formulation from the structural perspective uses the understanding of the mental structures that allow the psyche to maintain some level of balance in the face of internal as well as external stressors.

The therapeutic change in the formulation focuses on an increased capacity for the individual to take responsibility for their behaviour as well as to become more capable, aware and flexible.

Additionally, the so-called structural theory; is clear about the limits to change as well because we're all performing a balancing act between conflicting demands.

Yet if the ego is strengthened and the superego is weakened or reduced. Then a more effective, satisfied as well as less self-defeating balance can be achieved.

When we consider a formulation from the structural perspective, we could ask:

- What are the person's characteristic defences? Their benefits as well as costs?
- What's the client's capacity for self-reflection? Can they think about their internal states as well as motivation in a 'psychological' way?
- How able is the person to regulate their emotion?
- Is the person able to regulate and sustain their self-functioning? Do they have stable ideas, goals and values?

Adaptive perspective:

Moving onto our final perspective, we're going to discuss the Adaptive Perspective. Therefore, a formulation that uses this perspective sees mental health conditions as a process of mismatch between the person and the environment.

I think this interesting idea alone should make you want to read more.

In addition, the environment provides limited solution to the conflicts and this in turn limits the client's creative responses to life's challenges as well as this makes the conflicts self-confirming as they prevent the client from learning from their experience.

As always, I love to breakdown the psychology talk into easier chunks. So, this perspective believes that the environment around you makes it more difficult for you to deal with life's struggles, as well as make responses to make your life easier. In turn, these difficulties are self-confirming.

For instance, if you're a socially anxious person and you are in a crowd. Then the crowd makes it difficult to find a solution to deal with your struggle. Making your social anxiety self-confirming as you're anxious in crowds because you act anxious in crowds as the environment, the crowd, makes it difficult to find a solution. So, you become anxious.

Finally, this perspective sees change as the process of opening up the client to a wide range of creative options and breaking out of maladaptive cycles.

Overall, change is about helping the client to create better ways to deal with the struggles and break their bad habits or cycles of destructive behaviour.

Consequently, from the adaptive viewpoint, the formulation should ask:

- What patterns are the client repeating in these life problem or symptom and what is the unconscious aims?
- Why has this pattern arisen now or why Is the pattern intolerable now?
- What maladaptive cycles are occurring to maintain the pattern? Also, how are the client's response's distorting and changing their experience of life to make this pattern self- confirming.
- How do these stereotypical patterns prevent the individual from developing and achieving in life?
- What methods work well and the benefits their life?

Personally, I love this perspective because it focuses on the relationship between the environment and the person, as well as it shifts 'blame' of the symptoms and presenting behaviour away from the client. Which is always good as a lot of the time it isn't the client's 'fault' for their mental health difficulties.

CHAPTER 5: IMPORTANCE OF DIFFERENT PRESPECTIVES, SCINEIFITIC-NESS AND KEY CHARACTERISTICS

Throughout this section, I've shown you the different perspectives you can take within the psychodynamic approach. Although, if you've read any of my other books then you know that I love a holistic approach to psychology.

This is where you don't try to find a single cause of a behaviour, and instead you consider the all the possible causes of the behaviour. For example, looking at a behaviour through the cognitive, biological and sociocultural approach is holistic.

And the psychodynamic approach is no different because whilst it is true that a common element of all psychodynamic perspectives is the searching of themes as well as patterns. You need to consider the different perspectives in a formulation.

As a result, each perspective gives you a new area to

search and a new angle to understand your client from.

Additionally, you have multiple themes and patterns from different perspectives then this can increase a formulation's validity- and ultimately help the formulation to be as useful to the client as possible.

The Scientific-Ness of The Psychodynamic Approach:

I see you rolling your eyes behind the page, but relax I'm not going to lecture you about the problems of this approach. Yet I need to at least comment on the topic in terms of formulation.

Therefore, whilst the 'scientific' part of this approach presents us with a problem. It is not the client's conscious reaction and information that we're interested in. Instead it's the client's unconscious content that we want so we can intercept it through the difference perspectives.

Overall, this is a subtle process with large room for error. This potential is only increased when we are given very little case material about the individual, along with no data on the client's responses, or the therapist's level of experience to their interpretation.

I know these negatives sound bad but I may not always agree with the psychodynamic approach. Yet I have to say that it's one of the approaches I like researching, because you have to admit it is pretty interesting and sometimes just plain bizarre!

Key Characteristics of A Psychodynamic Formulation:

To wrap this very long chapter up, the psychodynamic approach to formulation emphasises the unconscious and sees the client's life problems and symptoms as expressing an underlying disorder in the individual's emotional life that arises from conflicting relationships, feeling, fears as well as desires.

Also, this approach identifies these conflicts as repeating across different contexts and are managed by defensive strategies that result in maladaptive cycles and these can become self-conforming.

Finally, these conflicts relate to the person's developmental history, major past relationship and attachment patterns.

In other words, the approach places a large amount of emphasis on childhood experiences.

PART THREE: SYSTEMIC FORMULATION

CHAPTER 6 SYSTEMIC FORMULATION

Moving onto our next interesting type of formulation, we're going to be looking at systemic formulation.

In short, systemic therapists view the family as a system of emotions with the feeling and thoughts all the people in the system influencing it heavily.

Meaning that if one person has a problem in the family or couple then this problem creates a ricochet effect throughout the entire system.

Systemic Formulation:

The systemic approach regards all aspects of the therapy as an interactional collaborative process, as well as formulation is something the therapist does with the family, not does to the family.

This type of formulation is co-constructional as therapist, team and family come together jointly to create new formulation to the problem.

The what, when, how of questioning is all seen as a way to bring significant change to the family.

The carefully crafted moment by moment feedback, questioning as well as eliciting fresh information for family members to consider is what Tomm (1987) called: 'integrative interviewing'

This leads to the formulation; as a process; slowly starting to shape the relationship within the family.

As a result, there's less assessment formulation interventive stages then in other therapies.

Interestingly, one of the early ideas in systemic thinking was that the symptom served as a function for stabilising the family.

However, this may sound counter-intuitive but it links to one of the first phase of proposed by the mental research Institute Research (Watzlawick et al, 1974) that consists of the video that problem arise from applying failing solution to the problem.

Exploration of the Problem:

In this stage, this is were the problem is explored in greater detail and a number of different aspects of the problem are explored.

Such as:

- What's the problem?

- How does the problem try to solve the difficulty?
- What worked and what didn't and evaluate?
- Discuss the family beliefs about the problem and what they do about them.
- Find out what decision were made about the problem and solution and which ones to purse.

With the exploration of the problem seeing description and formulation as having an 'as if' quality to them, because of the constructivist idea were personal meaning and experience are central to human activity. This led to formulation and assessment being seen not as a one-off scientific process but an ongoing dynamic process of developing, testing, and revising different formulations.

Personally, I fully agree with this idea about formulation because as you'll see through this book. Formulation should, at least in my opinion, be co-constructed and developed with the client.

Mainly, as a result of the therapist brings their expertise to the therapy. But the client brings their expertise in themselves and their life to the therapy.

Progressive Hypothesizing:

When I first heard of this type of hypothesizing, I have to admit that I found it odd. But as you'll soon see this is a great idea.

Therefore, Palozzoli et al (1978) also known as the Milan team of family therapists suggested the very useful idea that therapy and formulation are intertwined as well as they progress through the process of hypothesizing.

The reason why this idea is rather useful is because there is no such thing as an objective family truth, as families are unique systems that work in their own way to deal with a specific difficulty.

As a result, the closest you can come to a 'truth' is formulating a hypothesis and testing it out, as well as measuring its effectiveness to bring about positive change.

For example, if I believed that a client's difficulties were the result of the parents' constantly arguing and causing the high levels of distress to the client. Then I would test this hypothesis by focusing on the parents, getting them to argue less and seeing if this decreased distress bought around positive change for the client.

Another benefit of progressive hypothesizing is it helps the therapist not to be overwhelmed.

This is a real risk to therapists because families represent a lot of information at all different levels. Like: the interpersonal as well as individual level.

Thus, the hypothesis helps them to cut out some of the information so they can focus on one aspect of the client's difficulties before moving onto another aspect.

Furthermore, this hypothesizing helps to add direction to the therapy as well as this helps to reduce anxiety of initial contact with the family. This anxiety can be considerable for everyone involved, not least the therapist as they're in charge of 'fixing' or helping the client and the family.

Key Features:

A key feature of systemic formulation is it's elaborative and the therapy should elicit more information from the family.

This links to Cecchin (1987) who preferred formulation compared to creative curiosity as in formulation we're not testing for scientific truth- and the therapist encourages positive curiosity towards family.

In other words, you could propose that systemic formulation is about trying to explore and discover information the family system and its member. Prior to you using this information to inform your formulation.

Another key feature in systemic formulation is there's less pressure for the therapist to get it right as this is about elaboration and eliciting information from the family.

Finally, the systemic approach to formulation helps to reveal differences within the family that can impede therapy if left unstated.

Such as, if the client and their brother had a problem or difficulty creating tension. Then this tension could impede the therapy. So, discovering this tension and resolving it could be extremely important.

CHAPTER 7: FAMILY THERAPY, CONSTRUCTS, MODELS AND KEY CHARACTERISTICS

In a few chapters time, you'll learn a lot more about social constructivism but this section should still be easy to understand.

In modern systemic therapy, we are moving towards social constructivism. This is an extension of constructivist ideas that emphasize language and culture.

Due to language, whether spoken, written or signed, is not only the way we see the world but create meaning as well as construct it.

These are dominant ideas that a culture has and these dominant ideas influence the culture's and by extension , the family's ideas and perception. Such as: what makes a good mother and a good son.

Therefore, systemic therapy tries to bring these ideas into the family's conscious, so they are aware and not as constrained by them.

For instance, if a mother and her son were having difficulties because they were consciously or unconsciously punishing or restraining themselves because of a culture's ideas of a good mother, a good son and what a man should be.

It's important to make the client's aware of these influences so they can possibly be unrestricted.

In turn, this could reduce the difficulties between the two- without a real case to look at it's hard to give you anything more concrete.

Finally, this idea emphasises a more collaborative approach to the therapy whether the therapists and client's work side by side in a more open and transparent way.

Use of Self-Reflective Formulation:

Therapists bring their professional as well as personal experience to the formulation as a process.

In addition, the relationship between the therapist and client, therapist and the consulting team are deemed as very important to formulation.

Personally, I really like this feature or use of formulation because I have always believed in the importance to take into account the therapist's personal experience.

Therefore, this highlights the importance of the self-reflective stance as we all need to consider how we're going to affect the formulation and by extension the success of the therapy.

A Proposed Model of Systemic Formulation:

Despite systemic therapy evolving with an emphasis on pattern and structure to a therapy based on meanings. There are a number of common meanings. There are a number of common threads that can be drawn out to form a model of systemic formulation.

For example, here are a number of common threads within systemic formulation:

- They destruct the problem.
- Look for problem-maintaining patterns as well as feedback loops.
- They look at emotions, transitions, and attachments.
- They look at contextual factors

Building upon this to include social constructivism and an emphasis on cultural as well as language contexts (Dallos and Draper, 2010) It is important to consider the following 2 interconnected ideas.

- Analysis- exploration of family, understanding each other their problems, patterns and attempts to solve them. This happens throughout the process.

- Synthesis- works alongside or after assessment and analysis. This is where the therapist starts to integrate information to form hypothesises.

Overall, the ideas of analysis and synthesis are interdependent.

Remember:

The process of systemic formulation is an active, on-going one as well as therapists try to interpret the problem so they can come up with a hypothesis.

Finally, this type of formulation is about working with the family and it emphasises collaboration as a part of this dynamic process.

Key Characteristics of Systemic Formulation:

To wrap up this section, here are the key characteristics of a systemic formulation:

- The difficulties don't lay within the individual. They lay within the relational processes.
- Systemic formulation is centrally concerned with exploring meaning exception and understanding the family members in relation to the client's problems.
- Formulation is progressive hypothesising.
- There is no clear distinction between exploration, formulation, intervention.
- Formulation is about promoting the client.

- Formulation is collaborative.

Family members may have a range of conflicts that are very different. So, it's up to the therapist to try and gain a 'true picture' from the range of formulations.

CHAPTER 8: FORMULATION AND NARRATIVE THERAPY

Originally, I thought Narrative Therapy was writing about your difficulties and this writing would allow you to be rageful on the page. Ultimately, allowing you to heal.

Whilst this is NOT what Narrative Therapy is, I still highly recommend the above technique because after something tragic happened to me in my own personal life. Writing about it helped me to see that the event or series of unfortunate events were not my fault. Ultimately, this allowed me to heal and move on.

Narrative Therapy:

Moving onto the real therapy, Narrative therapy seeks to help people find their values, skills and knowledge that will allow them to effectively confront their problems.

Furthermore, the therapist seeks to help the client

write a new narrative about themselves by looking at the history of these skills, values, and knowledge.

Interestingly, Narrative Therapy claims to be a social justice approach to therapeutic conversations as it seeks to challenge dominant ideas that the therapy claims shape people's lives in destructive ways.

This is an interesting thought because sometimes using the phrase disorder and making the person change themselves can be destructive.

Finally, whilst narrative therapy is typically used in the field of family therapy. A lot of authors and practitioners report using these ideas and practices in community work, schools, and higher education with success.

Formulation in Narrative Therapy:

Typically, formulation is seen as an explanation for the causes of a client's difficulties and this positions the therapist as a technical expert.

Yet this represent a challenge for social constructivist views? (Harper and Moss, 2003)

(We'll look at Social Constructivism later in the book)

Furthermore, do formulations have to be about problems, causality history and more?

Interestingly, Carr (2012) proposed an idea that

highlights if therapists make a formulation ana analysis based on problems then our perspective will focus on finding a solution.

Initially, this hardly sounds like a bad thing, but this prospective leads to the therapist expecting there to be a problem. Even when there isn't a problem.

In addition, this solution focused perspective or expectation of problems could potentially lead to an interactional process that sustains the problem in the client's life.

As a result, Ducan Moss and David Harper suggested a process based on on-going collaborative sense making and not developing semi or completely objective description of problems.

This is very similar to progressive hypothesis from the last chapter.

Meaning formulations are situated in certain contexts as well as oriented to particular purposes- also known as perspectives.

For example, if you had two depressed people that were clinically the same. But they were from two completely different socioeconomic backgrounds. Then the formulation would focus more on the contexts instead of the clinical 'problem.'

What is Formulation in Narrative Therapy?

In narrative terms, clinical work can be seen as a series of dialogues or conservations.

Harper and Moss (2003) describes formulation as seeing a person's story's (despite it being authored in collaboration with the client) of that observation.

Building upon this further, Bob (1999), Parry and Doan (1994) as well as Corrie and Lore (2010) described formulation as a structured story that not only explains the way things are but how and what might need to happen in the future to facilitate change.

The benefit of this description of formulation is this orient the therapist and the client towards finding a way forward. As well as the formulations are made together and constructed instead of magically created and the client is forced to fit into the created formulation.

Personally, I like Narrative Therapy and formulation because it focuses on people's stories, and we all have our own unique story and shaped us into the people we are today. (Yes, I know genetics played a part as well)

Therefore, I think it's great that a therapy focuses on our individual stories and I truly appreciate the focus on how or what might need to happen so the change can occur in the future.

Key characteristics of formulation in narrative therapy:

Overall, formulation in narrative therapy is seen as a story developed together by therapists as well as clients using their own words and language as much as possible.

Also, these stories are not intended to be casual explanations of the difficulties.

Instead, the aim of the formulation is to encourage development of richly textured 'thick' multiple stories of people's lives.

In simpler terms, this might include:

- Describing externalised problems and identifying tactics it uses to exert people.
- Identity new maps and knowledge to scaffold emerging of new stories. Such as: ways created to live around the problem.
- Responses of others.
- Get creative and use careful and appropriate humour. Reconnect significant relationships from the client's past that help to sustain alternative previously 'hidden' stories
- Record of choices the client has made in relation to places of these stories and relationships in their lives.

CHAPTER 9: FORMULATION AND SOCIAL INEQUALITIES

I have to admit the first time I came across this approach to formulation I found it weird, strange as well as just plain confusing.

Mainly, because I had never ever heard of such a thing. The same applies to the Personal Construct Psychology section.

However, what I love about research. Whether it be for this book, my blog or my podcast is that I am always learning as well as developing my knowledge base.

Leading me to discover new interests and this strange area of psychology is actually rather interesting as you'll now see.

What is this Approach to Formulation?

The social inequalities approach to formulation is an approach that goes beyond the boundaries of psychology, at least the traditional boundaries; by empahising the role of social as well as cultural factors in the client's difficulties.

Additionally, this approach sees these factors in two different ways.

Firstly, the approach sees social and cultural factors as structural. That systematically marginalise some but not others.

In the field of psychology, this is viewed as part of the ideological dimension. This shapes how we think, feel and behave.

Including what we think is acceptable and deviant behaviour. For instance, what mental 'ill health' is.

How Does this Approach Apply to the Real World?

In the real world, social workers and other professionals can use this approach to formulation to try and deal with these divisions and the difficulties' consequences.

Yet what sets this approach as distinctive compared to other therapists is that most therapeutic solutions only tend to focus on the inter-personal or intrapsychic level.

In other words, it completely ignores societal factors that could be maintaining or even causing the client's problems.

Overall, the social inequalities perspective is about society's structure where it empowers some groups of people. Whilst it disempowers others.

Resulting in creating points of conflict between groups of people due to social injustices.

In other words, these social injustices can create psychological distress. Leading to difficulties for the client.

How Do You Define Social Inequalities?

This is difficult to answer because of the range of personal opinions on the topic but over the course of the next few sections. You should get a very good sense of what social inequalities are.

In fact, on the next page, I give you a lot of examples of social inequalities.

Interestingly, we can use social inequalities to figure out or map out the impact of social inequalities on people's mental health.

Personally, I think is very important as this provides us with the opportunity to study the effects of social inequalities on people. Meaning we have the data to 'prove', or something along those lines, the hypothesis about social inequalities having a negative impact on mental health.

Hopefully, allowing us to attempt to fix these social

inequalities and improve the mental health of people.

Social Inequalities and Mental Health:

Unequal distribution of social as well as economic resources in a society is crucial to explaining why some groups are more likely to seek help from psychological services. (Fryer, 1998)

For example, 'low' status groups experience the most negative and disempowering contact with services. (British Psychological society, 2008, 2012)

This is an interesting point I think because it is a bit confusing and this could create a negative cycle. As these 'low' status groups are more likely to experience psychological distress then they go to seek professional help. Only to be revictimized or go through even more distress.

To me that's just weird and futile.

As psychologists and therapists are there to stop or relieve the client's suffering- not add to it.

Takeaway:

I know the last section was a bit ranty, but I want to point out that we need to challenge inequalities when we encounter it.

I know this is easier said than done and we are all guilty of maintaining inequalities. I am no exception.

However, if you take anything away from this chapter in the book then please question and challenge people and yourself when you encounter social inequalities.

Examples of Inequalities:

Below are some examples of the different types of inequalities that can influence clients as well as could create distress and their difficulties.

Structural Inequalities: (Soico-Cultural Context)

- Gender
- Race
- Age
- Sexuality
- Class

Interpersonal Context/ Inequalities:

- Relationships
- Family
- Social role
- Economic role
- Solidarity:
- Community
- Participation
- Social support
- And more inequalities

Critical Evaluation Of Evidence Base:

Moving onto the evaluation of this approach, we need to discuss whether or not this approach is grounded in ideology or empirical evidence.

'Bio-Bio-bio model masquerading as the biopsychosocial model' (Boyle, 2002; Read et al, 2009)

Personally, I love this quote and I've written various versions of it throughout the book because I believe it's so important that we need to move firmly away from the biomedical model. I'll discuss why more throughout the book.

Basically, this perspective focuses on social and cultural factors in an individual's life that the other traditional perspective do not.

It questions the evidence base as well. Since the evidence-based approach, like the scientist practitioners; excludes or minimise the impact of sociocultural factors.

Again, I am a big supporter of the evidence-based approach as I think it's dangerous. If we start to deviant from the evidence. But I would like to stress, we need to include the effects social and cultural factors have on us. As these are massive and influential factors just like biological and cognitive factors are.

Furthermore, this perspective questions the evidence base as it questions the research design, stakeholder interest as well as publication bias in presentation of evidence in NICE, for example.

I think this is a relatively fair point to question as publication bias is a problem in psychology and sometimes the interest of stakeholders, I'm not talking about the interests of the client and the therapist, affect the therapy or the service more than it should.

Finally, this approach is valid as it's based on the relationship between social inequalities and mental health as well as other health conditions.

Also, it turns out this relationship has been extensively documented by many organisations.

Such as: BPS (2008), Department of Health (2010, 2009) and UNICEF (2011) to name a few.

Power and Inequalities:

Interestingly, this perspective adds another aspect to the critical social approach. This is the attention of dominant ideologies or discourses with traditional formulations that masks or tries to legitimatize inequalities, sustain and maintain power imbalances. (William, 1999) as well as misdirect our attention (Newsies, 2012) so we don't pay attention to these ideals or discourses.

However, mental health disciplines and professionals aren't only key sites to produce these discourses but they great places to contest them as well.

Therefore, this approach argues that as we are formulating, we are in a position to subtly control things. Through the process of medication, diagnosis and theory. All to the same end.

CHAPTER 10: KEY CHARATERISTICS OF THE SOCIAL INEQUAUTILIES

After looking at this topic or approach in depth, here are the summarised points for a formulation from the social inequalities perspective:

- The formulation provides opportunities for recognition as well as respect.
- Making mental realities and relevant social contexts visible.
- Critical consciousness about the presence of ideologies and domain discourse that lead to obscuring inequalities.
- Mapping of significant events as well as reactions overtime.
- While, acknowledging abilities, resources mapping reactive and survival shortage alongside oppressions and misuses of power.

- Pay attention to language differences of position and sense making.
- Recognise difference but do not 'other' them.
- You need to situate personal account with the wider socio-political narratives.
- Recognise that embodiment is a psychosocial process where oppressive practices are internalised and interact with identifying formulation.
- This formulation is centred around the client.
- Don't be disempowering
- The real test of a formulation from this perspective is to see if a formulation does the following: promotes peacital, respectful as well as equalities process that allow people to have a meaningful impact into their lives.
- The client is active in the formulation
- The formulation promotes respect for diversity, and it addresses social injustices.

My Final Thoughts:

I know that I was a bit ranty in certain passages of this section, but I find this approach interesting. Because it highlights that as future psychologists, we are in a position to challenge these inequalities.

Consequently, I know I am, and hopefully you are too, at least aware of these inequalities in psychology now- and hopefully we can challenge these in the future.

PART FIVE: FORMULATION IN PERSONAL AND RELATIONAL CONSTRUCT PSYCHOLOGY

.

CHAPTER 11: FORMULATION IN PERSONAL CONSTRUCT PSYCHOLOGY

Whilst I was researching this book, this was probably the fourth approach to formulation I came across- and I was CONFUSED.

As a result, I had never ever heard of personal or construct psychology before.

Therefore, this chapter was a major learning experience for me and hopefully by the end of this chapter, you will find it as interesting as well as useful as I did.

Personal Construct Psychology:

This type of psychology was originally developed by American psychologist George A. Kelly as well as his approach to human behaviour proposed that people are scientists. Due to everyone is constantly involved in a process of inquiry.

In addition, during this process people make a hypothesis about the world and they are constantly having their hypothesis validated and individualised.

Much like 'true' scientists, people become attached to their hypothesis. Allowing them to experience different emotions when their theories are reformulated.

In therapy, the therapist and the client are already in formulation as they try to figure out as well as hypothesize the current situation.

Personally, I think this approach is interesting if not a little weird. But this approach makes logical sense due to humans are always trying to figure out the world around them.

Also, humans do tend to make predictions or they ideas about how the social world works. You only need to talk to a friend to consider why two people did something to see this in action.

For example, you and your friend get together to talk about why X and Y had a fight.

This is a perfect example of people hypothesizing about the world.

Overall, Personal Construct Psychology or PCP comes under constructivism.

Definition:

Personal Construct Psychology can be defined as 'the study and application of how human beings create systems of meaning in making sense of and acting in the world'

Additionally, a distinguishing feature of PCP is the belief that we develop a bipolar construct about our current situation.

Meaning in a situation, we experience and see the situation in terms of similarities and differences, and we move along this pole.

Overall, the ends of the pole help to govern our actions in regard to the situation.

For example, if the situation is similar to our hypothesis then people may say we are in a state of happiness.

Personal Construct Formulation:

Moving onto the formulation part of this section, a personal construct formulation is central to Kelley's Approach. Despite the formulation being regarded as coming from the cognitive behavioural tradition of psychology. (Brunch, 1998)

Additionally, there are two approaches to formulations. These are the structuralism and constructivist approaches. (Kelley, 1955: 454)

Structuralism:

Firstly, a structuralism formulation is tentative to the client and the therapist clinically organises the structured information for future reference.

This allows the therapist to look at the client from the view of 'normal' society as well as the viewpoint from the client.

For example, if a client is considered delusional by a normal viewpoint. It may be important to note that the client's view keeps referring to something about a family problem.

If this is the case then this could be a good takeaway and something to investigate later on in the formulation.

Constructivism:

This second approach to formulation is where the therapist organises the information in terms of the client's internal personal constructs.

Afterwards, the therapist construes or subsumes these internal constructs. This is where the therapist steps into the client's shoes. Making sure they don't bring their own personal biases with them.

Although, it is worth noting that having a client's constructs provide invalid could be a traumatic experience If these constructs are central to the person's view of the self. (Leitner, 1988)

It's just something to consider if you're ever going to do such a thing because you need to invalid them sometimes. So, you need to be careful and help the client through this difficult time.

<u>Diagnostic constructs:</u>

Whilst this section could be a 3,000 word essay in itself, I just wanted to mention that this approach to formulation doesn't use the typical diagnostic labels.

Therefore, I encourage you research it outside of this book to see what Kelley used instead.

For example, Kelley doesn't use the term interpersonal relationships in his approach. Instead he calls them sociality.

These constructs are how Kelley thought all you could see the client's construct as well as sociality through their eyes.

CHAPTER 12: CONSTRUING

Within this approach to formulation, Kelley places a high emphasis on construing. In short, this is how people think about the world as well as this is almost identical to the idea of the cognitive unconscious.

Covert Construing:

Whilst Kelley didn't use the term unconscious. He did use the term 'at a low level of cognitive awareness'

Consequently, some of the client's predicament may be down to convert construing so it's the aim of therapy to increase the level of awareness.

Structure of Construing:

Interestingly, different personal constructs differ in importance to different people. As a result, constructs are hierarchical in nature.

Furthermore, research shows that the most important constructs are the most resistant to change (Hinkle, 1965)

Meaning it is best not to challenge these constructs at in the early stages of therapy.

Strategies of construing:

In fact, there is no one way for people to construe about the world so people use different strategies to make sense of the world.

Now, some of these strategies are polar opposites of one another but two strategies are:

- Dilation- incompatible construct extend perceptual field to reorganise construct system at a more comprehensive level.
- Polar opposite- constructive- people perceptual field to minimize incompatibility in construing.

This polar opposite strategy runs the risk of overwhelming and threatening the person with anxiety.

- Dependency

Moreover, Kelley (1955) viewed a person's optimal functioning as a involving wide base of dependency relationships.

A problem can occur if a person is only dependent on small number or large number of people for problems.

Whilst this idea isn't a principal axis of Kelley's system. It still could be an important aspect of the formulation for a client's difficulties.

Personally, I see his idea of dependency as a social support network.

Content of Construing:

When it comes to the content of a person's view about the world, Kelley believed that there is no one right way to see the world, and I can understand and appreciate that.

Also, Kelley thought that a mental condition could arise of the construct's context and not the personal constructs themselves.

To simplify this idea, an example would be when the social factors and the biological factors interact to form depression for the person. Despite the person having a positive view of the world.

This was a quick example.

Overall, a personal construct formulation will still consider the client context of their construing as this allow the therapists to know which pathways are open to the client. In turn, this allows or helps the therapist to explain their choices.

Additionally, this formulation could identify conflicts posed by logical constructs in the client's construing.

For instance, when a client's construct is the preferred pole of construct and the non-preferred pole of another.

For example, if the client says "I don't want an eating disorder. I want to be slim but people with eating disorders are slim,"

This is a clear example of a logic conflict as this client believes that you need to have a eating disorder to be slim.

Note: like all examples in this book, they are purely fictional and you should not use them as medical, legal or professional advice under any circumstances.

Extra note:

Kelley's approach has provided us with the basis for personal construct formulation for a wide range of different conditions as well as many of these are supported by research findings.

This has led to evidence-based personal construct therapeutic approaches for these construing. (Winter, 1992; Winter and Vimey, 2005)

Ways to Assess Personal Constructs:

Finally, there are many different ways to assess a client's personal constructs.

For example, you can interview them to see their

views on the world and if they are distorted.

Equally, you could get them to take part in self-characterisation. This is where they write a character in third person as if this is by someone who knows you very well.

Finally, you can use Repertory grid techniques. This is an interview technique where you measure aspects of the client's personality. Also, you use qualitive grids and the 'bowtie' grid. This is a powerful tool for mapping a person's inter-constructs by using the client's own language to questions and mapping out their responses in a grid.

CHAPTER 14: KEY CHARACTERISTICS

As always here's your summary of the key characteristics of a formulation in this approach.

- PCP assumes people are always formulating constructs about their world, as well as these constructs are open to being replaced by alternative constructs.

- This type of formulation recognised that a person's experience of feelings and difficulties are shaped as well as structured by the way how they are construed.

- Formulations are based on good understand of how the client is construing about their situation and the other figures in their life.

- Therapists are encouraged to see the world through the client's eyes by taking a credulous, when the therapist is too ready to believe thing, and accepting approaching towards their client's beliefs and views.

- PCP provides diagnostic constructs and assessment methods.

- Formulation doesn't only have to consider the client but social construing as well.

- And not only monadic but dyadic as well as triadic construing as well.

- Formulations should be loosely held with openness to unique situations and construing predicaments.

- Finally, this approach to formulation places a high emphasis on reflexivity. This is where the therapist takes their own beliefs, thoughts, and behaviours into consideration to minimise their impact on the therapy.

PART SIX: INTEGRATIVE APPORACH

CHAPTER 15: WHAT IS THE INTEGRATIVE APPROACH?

Extremely similar to a future chapter on formulation where I go into my love for the topic of Team Formulations. This is a chapter that I have a soft spot for because I love as well as fully believe in the integrative approach to formulation.

In short, this is where you as the therapist draw on multiple models and you integrate them into one model.

From there, you pull on the parts of each therapeutic model that you selected, and you use them to create a more holistic formulation for the client.

Personally, I love this approach because as you'll see through this book and the next chapter. There are a lot of advantages to using different parts of each model.

What is this Approach?

To help us understand this approach in more depth. Here is an extract from Abnormal Psychology 2nd Edition.

Note: Eclecticism is another term for the integrative approach.

"Eclecticism is an approach to treatment that pulls together and weaves multiple types as well as forms of therapy together. (Beitman, Goldfriend and Norrcross, 1989)

An example of this eclecticism is Linehan's Dialectical Behaviour Therapy (DBT) for borderline personality disorder because this therapy weaves the cognitive, behavioural and humanistic as well as psychodynamic approaches together.

This approaches to therapy is great because it offers the therapist flexibility to propose and follow enquires and back away from ineffective approaches and this allows the therapist to find the different causes of the disorder. As different approaches target differences causes.

In my opinion, this is a great idea for therapists because I was talking to my Lecturer at University about this and she completely agreed with me when I said that this is a great idea. As surely if a therapist only uses one type of therapy or approach to treatment then this can harm the effectiveness of the treatment.

In addition, she added as well that in the United Kingdom at least when you're doing your clinical placement also known as your doctoral training. You train in three different models or types of therapy.

For example, I think that my lecturer trained in Cognitive Behavioural Therapy, Psychodynamic Therapy and Systematic Therapy.

For more information on these types of therapies, please check out my <u>Clinical Psychology</u> book."

<u>The Models:</u>

In theory, you can combine, mix and match whatever models of therapy you want.

However, in reality, therapists choose models to combine based on evidence supported and/or work in practice (Wachtel, 1991)

In other words, if there's no evidence interpersonal conflicts or difficulties then you wouldn't combine systemic therapy with your other choices as systemic therapy wouldn't be useful to you. As this operates at the interpersonal level.

Confusion about Eclecticism:

Although, it was be noted that there is a fair amount of confusion or mystery surrounding Eclecticism to some extent.

As a result of Eclecticism is implied by professional guidelines, but these guidelines don't specify how to synthesize this approach.

Meaning the guidelines don't help the therapist to make sense and combine the results of these different models.

Nonetheless, while there is no official name. The therapist is likely to come from one of the following positions.

Firstly, a therapist can choose to try and match a diagnosis or a client's symptoms to a therapy.

For example, if a client has a diagnosis of depression then the therapist may wish to match them to a therapy of CBT.

Secondly, the therapist could consider either an exploratory approach to combining therapies or they could choose to use only scripted therapies. Like Cognitive Behavioural Therapies.

Finally, this approach to an integrative formulation can be described as drawing on the medical or drug metaphor (Stiles and Shapio, 1994)

This is where the approach pretends people are the active ingredients as well as it assumes the validity of diagnosis system.

CHAPTER 16: HOW TO CHOOSE MODELS?

This is a critical question because if you as the therapist choose the wrong models to base your formulation on. Then at best you're wasting time and at worse you're probably causing harm to the client. Due to the increased psychological distress of the client believing the therapy isn't working. Or they are simply unfixable.

To help you decided which models to use, you should consider the following:

- Developmental stage

Your approach to formulation will be based on therapeutic models that may suited to different people at different stages of preparedness for therapeutic intervention.

For example, if someone wants to change and better themselves. Then you will take a different approach to someone who doesn't think they're experiencing any difficulties.

For example, if someone isn't aware of their problems or difficulties then it tends to be best for therapists to use an exploratory approach.

- Contemplating stage

There is where there is some recognition and awareness of the difficulties as well as problems. But the client doesn't realise the full extent of the difficulties.

For clients at this stage, cognitive approaches tend to be best. Due to this approach investigates the underlying beliefs, conditional thoughts as well as feelings that could be holding back from next stage.

There are other stages to consider but these stages should be enough for now to get you thinking.

Collection of Techniques and Strategies:

Additionally, something that I love about the integrative approach to formulation is that it draws on different therapeutic models.

However, it draws on the techniques of these different models as well.

This is another way for therapists to choose what models they want to draw on because you might only want to use a technique of one approach without drawing on the theory.

For example, there is one multimodal approach by Lazarus (2005) that we're look at now.

So, therapist can use techniques from different approaches without using theories that created them.

Furthermore, below is an anagram, BASIC ID, for the different areas that a therapist should use to consider a client's problem from different angles.

- Behavior
- Affect (emotion)
- Sensation
- Imagery
- Cognition
- Interpersonal
- Drugs/beliefs

As previously mentioned, this is used to get therapists to consider intervention in these areas.

Meaning if you're client as difficulties related to cognition, behaviour and sensation. Then you pick techniques and focus on those areas more than the other areas.

Collection of Clinical Hypotheses

Finally, the two best-known examples of an integrative formulation are in this category.

For instance, Ingram (2006) provided an ambitious

list of 28 core hypothesis that embrace all theories as well as orientations within the discipline of psychology and psychotherapy.

Using the headings of loss, biological causes, levels of social support and more.

She describes it as a framework that summarises core ideas and not a conceptual synthesis of all the different models.

Leading us to ask the question of: How do you do a conceptual synthesis of the models?

Conceptual Synthesis:

A conceptual synthesis aims to achieve a theoretical integration to develop new and more effective models.

This is where I get very excited in my opinion because I love the idea of combining the old therapies to create something new and hopefully more effective. So, it can better the lives of the clients.

Moreover, a conceptual synthesis is likely to fall into one of the three categories, we're going to talk about.

Off the Shelf-Integrative Models:

These models use standardised integrative formats for all formulations. That outline detailed integrative frameworks that can be used as the basis of an integrative formulation as well as intervention.

In other words, this type of model is a basis for an integrative where you simply pick it up and you are start to use it.

One example of this model is Cognitive Analytic Therapy (Ryle, 1995) that combines models like personal construct therapy and object relation theory

Common Factor Integrations:

With these types of models, you search for more conceptions coherent integration. That is fuelled by the search for the active ingredients in the psychotherapies.

In short, this is what makes the psychotherapy work and it is that 'working' part of the therapy that is used.

A common example of this model is the therapeutic alliance because it is the integration of the relationship between the client and therapist, the degree of agreement with the aims of therapy and how to achieve change.

Idiosyncratic integration:

Finally, we have a truly interesting idea where over the years, professionals have made their own personal approaches, drawing on both different therapies and models.

For example, the Weerasekera framework.

CHAPTER 17: WEERASEKERA FRAMEWORK

This integrative approach by Weerasekera's (1995) model has two axis.

It focuses on the origins of the problem. Focusing on the individual and systemic/ relationships.

In addition, it includes the 4P framework and it draws on different therapeutic approaches. As well as this provides a framework for deciding on an intervention package.

As this model draws on systemic, attachment and narrative models of therapies. We're going to compare and contrast them.

Systemic Therapy:

Casting your mind back to the systemic formulation chapter, this therapy focuses on the family systems and the workings of the system.

A few weaknesses of the systemic model is:

- It only has a single application.
- The model doesn't make it clear why the client's condition develops.
- It isn't clear why certain people develop conditions and not others, and why each person has their own unique coping mechanisms.

Building upon this further, systemic therapy focuses on how family dynamics shape individuals, their intervention workings as well as their feelings and behaviour.

Also, a systemic formulation has less of a focus on how wider socioeconomic factor can impact the formulation.

Finally, a long standing weakness or controversy around systemic therapy is that it states whilst you're not blaming the client. Your are instead feeling up the blame to the family as well as the parents.

Narrative therapies:

Again, this is similar to systemic therapy but it focuses on the client's internal narratives. And it places a high emphasis on communication processes. (White and Espton, 1990 and Sluzki, 1992) as well as the therapy highlights the importance of meaning.

In terms of the meaning we give to life and events and how they shape our feelings as well as behaviour.

In contrast, the emphasis is on patterns and stories. But not the patterns in a client's actions or behaviours.

Attachment theory:

As a quick recap, attachment is the emotional bond between the client and a caregiver.

In addition, people use the caregiver or attachment figure as a secure base and for comfort.

Attachment and Systemic Process:

Now, both theories share an emphasis on patterns of interaction in the family, as well as how 'problems' may be functional responses to the dynamics of the family. This differs depending on the family style and the individual's attachment style.

Interestingly, Hill-burn- Cobb (1996) found that the structural family concepts of unrested and disengaged. Made or matched the individual attachment styles of ambivalent/ re-occupied and avoidant.

In much simpler words, he found that a family's style and a person's attachment style could match.

Finally, attachment and systemic models are important because formulations happen in sociocultural contexts, cultural frames. Meaning the way how the family sees psychological 'problems' and even the society's views are important in a formulation. As they will influence and impact it.

This is the same for structural constricts. Such as: function restriction on treatment types.

For example, if a family looks down upon anti-depressants then this will restrict treatment options for the client.

CHAPTER 18: KEY CHARATERISTICS AND GUIDING PRINICPLES

Overall, in an Integrative Formulation there are a number of key characteristics that help to set this approach to formulation apart from the others. Including:

- The formulation is regarded as a fluid dynamic process. As well as formulation is used as a verb.
- Different models can contribute to this dynamic and collaborative process.
- Formulation is a collaboration between the therapist and the client.
- Meaning the therapist and the client create the formulation together.
- This co-construction is the centre of this dynamic process.

Guiding Principles:

Additionally, there are guiding principles that must be used during an integrative formulation.

- The formulation is an active process.
- The personal meaning is the central integrating factor in a formulation.
- Personal development and integration are important.

Summary:

To summarise, in Integrative formulation, it is a process, intrinsic aspect of the therapeutic relationship.

Furthermore, formulation and reformulation are done sensitively, collaboratively with reflectivity.

Finally, it uses personal meaning as the central integrating factors and it links personal to professional development.

CHAPTER 19: INTERGRATIVE FORMULATION IN PRATICE

Following on from the last few chapters where we looked at the theoretical basis of the integrative approach to formulation. We'll now look at how you can apply theory to the real world.

Personally, I always like these sort of chapters due to the theory is interesting. However, it's always good to see what we learn has real world importance.

Formulation and Therapeutic Relationship:

In the integrative approach, formulation is rather unscientifically described as an interactive, fluid, vibrant activity.

During which we get to learn about the appearance and the uniqueness of our clients.

This is what I love about psychology and psychotherapy because we get to know the person, and we don't simply put them in a box.

Ultimately, this view offers professionals a basis for conceptualising an integrative formulation as well as it is the formulation development and maintenance of this formulation that are the core parts of this dynamic process.

In other words, by learning about the uniqueness of the client. It gives us a way to visualise the integrative formulation that we can develop as a part of a larger co-constructive process.

Speaking of the formulation process, formulation can be seen as occurring through several central processes.

Including our focus on the belief stories as well as feelings of the client. This is important so the client knows they are being understood and valued, as well as this helps psychotherapists to adapt the therapy to the client.

Another central process is attending to the nature of the interaction between the clients and therapist.

Also, therapists need to consider the external factors influencing our client.

Finally, the therapist needs to process their own beliefs as the interview unfolds. This is also known as reflexivity.

Putting the Integrative in Integrative Formulation:

As I've already mentioned in this book, I love integrative formulation so it's time we actually bring a few different approaches together.

Therefore, different models potentially make relative contribution to different formulations. This allows for different integrative combinations.

For example, as you'll see in a minute narrative therapy as well as systemic can be combined into a very effective integrative model.

Remember:

Nonetheless, the most importance to remember is formulation is subjective, an interpersonal process and everyone can give a different interpretation of the same client.

Consequently, formulation is up to the client and the therapist- depending on the model used. So, it's up to the therapist to pick and choose what models to use based on their feelings about the client.

Additionally, you might have two people with the exact same diagnosis, but the therapist may feel the need to use different models on them. This is fine.

If you become a therapist one day then trust yourself and your experience and do what is best for your client, and if you choose five models then choose them!

Attachment Narrative Therapy (ANT):

Showing an integrative model or formulation in practice, we'll look at Attachment Narrative Therapy.

This type of therapy is where the therapist provides a secure base of safety and exploration for the client. As discussed, my Bowlby's attachment theory.

In short, his work proposes that people fuse attachment figures as a secure base to explore the environment and to feel safe.

Please see Developmental Psychology 2nd Edition for more information.

Overall, ANT adds onto Bowlby's broad approach as well as it combines the narrative, systemic as well as individual models of therapies at both a theoretical and pragmatic level. To form an integrative model of therapy.

Additionally, Bowlby saw therapy as a process of creation and maintaining the secure base that people need for attachment, as well as Bowlby's theory is an ingredient of system theory.

Interestingly, Dallos and Vetere (2009) developed the approach to form a common framework to be used with a range of complex conditions. Ranging from ADHD to trauma to eating disorders.

Furthermore, the approach brings together a range of models that operate at different levels.

For instance, the narrative approach operates at the societal level, the systemic approach operates at the interpersonal level, as well as attachment theory operates on the individual level.

In my opinion, this is a great model because it works on multiple levels so you can understand the client and their difficulties more.

Therefore, you are more able to help them and tailor the treatment to them as you understand them more, as well as you can target the difficulties at these different levels.

Overall, ANT is on example of how different therapeutic approaches can contribute to an integrative framework.

Integration Based on A Conceptual Synthesis of Complementary Models:

Wow, that was a mouth full!

In this last section, you'll going to be learning about how to create or develop an integrative model of therapy.

Consequently, when you want to create a model, you need to start off with an awareness of the overlaps that exist between different models.

In other words, their compatibility.

For instance, you wouldn't want two approaches that focus on the client's difficulties at an individual level.

Instead, you would want two or more models that operate at different levels.

In addition, you need to be aware of the disadvantages of each model as well as these disadvantages need to be 'corrected' or at least balanced by another model.

For example, a disadvantage of CBT is that it doesn't focus on non-mental factors. Yet this can be balanced by combining this model with narrative therapy.

CHAPTER 20: INTERGRATIVE FORMULATION IN HEALTH SETTINGS

After looking at Integrative Formulations in the past few chapters, I wanted to end this section on applying this concept to health psychology and settings.

Personally, I would never go into health psychology, despite myself writing a small Health Psychology book, I want to respect the people who do what to go into Health Psychology.

Therefore, in a health setting, a biopsychosocial formulation will always be used.

As a result, you always need to consider how the biological, psychological and social factors interact to create the difficulty.

This is extremely important in health settings where you're treating physical problems.

Furthermore, formulations can be pro-active as well as preventive. Meaning that the formulation can happen before events that might cause an increase in psychologically distress had occurred.

Generally, team formulations are used and it seeks to incorporate the practical perspective of the wider healthcare team, and the client's views.

Although, formulations in a health setting don't typically fit or use the usual assessment-formulation-intervention model.

Due to these formulations may be more the reverse (intervention-formulation-assessment) and 'on the spot' as the medical intervention proceeds.

Using a completely fictional example if you wanted to do a formulation on a stroke victim. You could have to do the medical intervention first then the formulation to investigate the cause of the stroke then possibly medically assess the patient before discharge.

You could do a formulation on the stroke patient to see if stress was a factor in the stroke. This is what probably happened to my cousin a few months ago.

Finally, formulations in health settings are always integrative. As they address impact of the disease and the therapist has the ability to draw on theoretical constructs and ideas from health psychology and other therapeutic models. To make their formulation more accurate or 'correct.'

Noticed that I mentioned team formulations in this

chapter, I wonder how they work and why you might want to use them?

PART SEVEN: TEAM FORMULATIONS

CHAPTER 21: WHAT IS A TEAM FORMULATION?

In my opinion, you cannot beat team formulations and as you can probably tell I'm extremely excited to write about this topic.

Personally, I love team formulations as this feeds into the idea about being holistic, and if you're read the other books in the series then you know I'm a massive fan of holistic psychology.

This is where you don't try to reduce the cause of a behaviour down to a single cause. Instead you look at what causes the behaviour from multiple angles.

One example of this holistic approach, you want instead of looking exclusively at how the social factors influence your client's depression you would look at the cognitive, biological and interpersonal reasons as well.

Linking to team formulation, I love that team formulation allows you to pull on the strengths as well as professional and sometimes personal experiences of your team to help solve your client's difficulties.

Additionally, team formulations are recommended by HCPC (Health Professions Council, 2009) clinical psychology leadership framework (Skimmer and Toorgood, 2010) BPS and more professional organisations.

How can you Define Team Formulation?

The term team formulation can be broadly defined as co-constructing a team formulation in response to a particular request.

Basically, this is where the therapist asks for help.

Also, by requesting help and introducing team formulations this can be the first step to introducing regular formulation meetings.

We'll discuss these meetings in a moment.

CHAPTER 22: HOW TO USE A TEAM FORMULATION?

Once a psychologist wants to conduct a team formulation then they tend to do the following steps.

Firstly, they review the client's notes. This allows them to understand their client and their difficulties. As well as it means the psychologist can think of questions and areas that they want help with.

Afterwards, the psychologist can meet with key staff members to get their thoughts and feelings on the client.

Subsequently, using this knowledge the psychologist can draw up a tentative formulation.

In other words, this is a rough formulation or a draft.

Following this drawing up or drafting, the psychologist can setup a staff meeting to get feedback on the formulation from the other members of the team.

This is the feature I particularly like because it allows the psychologist to learn from the other members, as well as it helps you to draw on other models of therapy that you yourself may not be overly familiar with.

Next, the psychologist revises the formulation to an agreed upon version and the psychologists uses the formulation to develop a group or individual intervention plan.

Finally, you use a user friendly version of the formulation without all the psychobabble to the client, as well as you incorporate their feedback.

Source: Meaden and Van Marle (2008), Walton (2011) as well as Clarke (2008)

Again, another reason why I really appreciate team formulations is because they take a collaborative stance and work with the client as well.

Whilst team formulations may place less of an emphasis on the co-construct or collaboration side. At least, they try to incorporate the client's thoughts at the end.

Useful Concepts in Team Formulation:

Before, we move on any further here are some important concepts for psychotherapy as a whole but especially team formulation.

- Transference- where the client transfers their feelings to the therapist.

- Countertransference- where the therapists transfers their feelings to the client because the client reminds them as someone they know or knew. Or because of their own unresolved conflicts.

- Cycles of re-victimisation- the cycle of victimisation that can come from a number of sources including the service itself.

- Rescuer, persecutor, victim triangle- a toxic triangle of interpersonal relationships between people with one of more of these characteristics: helpless, judgement and critical (bully) and helpful but they always feel the need to be involved and wanted.

- Sick role bias- the therapist looks for a problem or mental condition because someone has come to them with a belief about a problem.

Benefits of Team Formulation:

This is an interesting question in my opinion because I can write as much as I want, and I can rave about team formulations. But without knowing the benefits of team formulations all the other pieces of information in this section is fairly pointless.

Although, I must confess upfront that the benefits of team formulations are under researched. Much like Individual case formulations.

Nonetheless, we can still find out some great benefits of team formulations.

For example, some studies show that the team approach to formulation has additional benefits compared to individual formulation. Such as: it can inform the intervention as well as it can clarify the formulation.

Moreover, the DCP (2011) states that team formulations have a lot of benefits. Like: they can help a psychologist to achieve a consistent team approach towards intervention.

Also, it can help the professional team, client and the carer work together so everyone gets want they want, and this helps the client with their difficulties.

It creates new ways of thinking; the professionals are supporting each other as well as this draws on and values all the team member's expertise.

This is a great benefit because it creates these new ways of thinking which the psychologist can use to inform future interventions to help future clients.

Also, I strongly believe in valuing everyone's expertise as you don't know everything so others can help you in the areas you aren't as familiar with.

Moreover, this raises staff morale and it helps the team to understand attachment styles in relation to the service as a whole.

I mention this benefit because sometimes clients use the therapist or the service as a secure base to feel safe and form an attachment with. like: I mentioned in the integrative section of the book.

This is important for the team to realise as it can inform the formulation as well as the service needs to be careful at the end of the intervention to prevent the client from losing a source of attachment.

If the service isn't careful then this could have devasting consequences further down the line.

Penultimately, team formulations can help to increase the team's understanding, empathy and reflectiveness. As a result of the team being involved in new cases, learning from new experiences and encountering new individual cases with their own trauma as well as difficulties.

Finally, a team formulation allows the service and the team to challenge unfounded 'myths' or beliefs about the service user.

For example, if you have a foster child as a service user who was aggressive then someone in your team believes that 'it's just how foster children are' then that's a very damaging belief.

Meaning you can challenge this belief at the team

meeting and discuss why the belief is wrong. You can draw on the service user's history to support you.

I mentioned this foster child example because I used to have a foster child who 'suffered' (hate that term) with ADHD and Autism as a best friend and there were a lot of negative false beliefs surrounding this person. So, it was my job to challenge these false beliefs.

Formulation Meetings:

As promised in this section, we'll discuss formulations and if you become a clinical psychologist or therapists, you will almost certainly attend one of these meetings in your career.

Formulation meetings are regular meetings for the whole team that are usually weekly.

Additionally, they were developed by Lake (2008), Down (2010) and more.

Occasionally when formulations are embedded in a service, the aim of formulation meetings were to provide all clients with a formulation. (Kennedy et al, 2003) and (Down, 2010)

The formulation meetings are typically designed into timeslots of up to 90 minutes.

How do Team Formulation Meetings Work?

Luckily, these meetings do have a typical format that facilitates a team formulation meeting very well.

Firstly, the team members review the background information as well as the reasons for the referral.

Then the psychologist develops a formulation with the team, as well as they outline possible interventions.

Before, the psychologist writes up the disseminated information.

I know I keep saying it throughout this section, but I am really looking forward to attending a team formulation meeting. Due to I believe it will be great to see professionals bounce ideas around, building upon each other's work and yes I'm not deluded that none of this probably happens in real meetings.

Instead, I can imagine a few meetings were there's a lot of infighting and senior professionals as well as professionals with differing models wanting to prove their 'right'.

If someone ever did that to me, I'll just point out there's no such thing as 'correct' or 'right' in psychotherapy.

Regardless of that, you'll see what I mean in the final section of the book.

The Facilitation Role in Meetings:

Within the above definition or use of team formulation, the facilitation role is not about providing a solution but to clarify, summarise reflect, encourage creativity, ask questions as well as encourage free thinking amongst the professionals.

These are all important skills to develop the professionals as well as to ensure that the psychologist has the 'best' formulation to help their client.

Building upon this further and this largely depends on the service where the therapist is employed, but these meetings tend to draw from a core model.

It's often Cognitive Behavioural Therapy. Kennedy (2008) Clarke (2008) and Ingham (2011) as well as sometimes it's the psychodynamic model of therapy (Devenport, 2002)

CHAPTER 23: TEAM FORMULATION AND INTEGRATION

It will probably come as no surprise to you that I'm going to be raving or as I like to put it reminding you about integrative formulations.

Due to it's an integrative formulation that makes me a fan of team formulations, as I strongly believe the entire point of these team formulation is to draw on the expertise of other professionals. This includes others that have expertise in different models.

The main reason being this allows you to use models that operate on different levels so you can be more holistic in your intervention as mentioned earlier.

Overall, it's important to use an integrative approach in team formulation for a few different reasons. Not including if your team all practice the same therapeutic model then it's possible that instead of helping and developing your intervention. It could harm it as the psychologist would be in an echo chamber.

Integrating Formulation into a Service:

This is an interesting idea where you or the profession tries to integrate formulation into the work of the service at every level.

Not only is this the ultimate aim for psychotherapy in some circles but this is extremely difficult as there's only one known example.

This example is an ambitious project in an older people's service in Tees Esk and Wear Valley NHS Foundation Trust. (Dexter- Smith, 2010)

At this psychological service provider, all staff members have been fully trained to implement formulation at all stages of the client's care. Using a formulation that is constructed with a CBT based diagram.

In turn, this CBT based formulation is supported by a range of materials. For example, Crib sheets templated to transfer formulation to an electronic system as well as accessible documents for staff to complete with the family and clients.

Additionally, the client's family as well as carers might be invited to attend a meeting. Allowing the service to gather information about the client's difficulties at different levels. Such as: interpersonal.

Yet Shirley (2010) points out that this decision must be carefully made as well as the advantages and disadvantages must be considered.

Finally, Carven-Staines et al's evaluation (2010) shows that despite positive feedback of formulation being rolled out. It has been difficult to implement on such a large scale as well as to implement this large-scale cultural change.

CHAPTER 24: THOUGHTS AND FORMULATION LETTER

Personally, I think this is a great idea in theory as it means that all clients can get access to a formulation that is tailor-made to them, their own difficulties as well as their own unique circumstances. Meaning that the most effective intervention can potentially be planned for them.

However, as much as I love this idea. I must confess that I doubt this would ever become the norm as much as we would like.

As a result of budget constraints and the sheer cultural changes that need to happen. As it's currently, a lot easier, and it saves the health care system time as well as money, to label someone with depression, give them a course of CBT and hope it works.

Although, I hope in time that this massive cultural change will help bring around the needed change so we can move away from the biomedical model or the bio, bio, bio model pretending to be the biopsychosocial model. Towards the biopsychosocial model being the normal, default model in services. Where we focus on the biological, cognitive and social factors of the client's difficulties.

Sure, it may take decades or even a few hundred years but hopefully, we will reach that goal one day.

Team formulation letter:

In our final section on team formulations, we need to talk about the all-important team formulation letter. This is the user-friendly explanation of the formulation that you give to the client.

Be Careful:

Whomsley (2009) pointed out that it isn't uncommon to feel as if the team are effectively talking behind the client's back.

This is why it's important to be careful about what you share with the client as you don't want to offend them. Also, you need the client to know that you are there for them.

PART EIGHT: CONTROVERSIES AND DEBATES

CHAPTER 25: CONTROVERSIES AND DEBATES AROUND FORMULATION

Personally, I love this next section because when I originally researched this book. I thought of this section as scary and overly dense.

However, once I started researching the problems as well as the debates within formulation. I actually fell in love with this section because it definitely gets you to start thinking.

Before, we go further into the chapter, I want to make it clear from the start that all theoretical principles and similar, that of the approaches, therapies and the like are built upon- are based on research and empirical data.

Therefore, I wanted to start off this section why starting with an easy debate around formulation.

Firstly, as a reader, you have probably found that formulations can be very overwhelming because there are so many ways to understand a single case.

As a result, each case could be taken from any of the approaches discussed in this book.

For example, if you have a client with an eating disorder. Do you do a Case Formulation? A Systemic? Narrative? Integrative? Team Formulation?

It's just a thought and even if you have the case details. You might be able to get rid of a few suggestions but... you will still have a long list of possible approaches to use.

Overall, a negative of formulation is that unlike diagnoses that gives you a clear concrete label. Formulation gives you a lot of overwhelming choices.

Consequently, if you as the reader are feeling overwhelmed about the choices available to you as a current or future therapist. Then I would like to remind you about taking an integrative approach where you may wish to draw on multiple approaches to your formulations.

Are Formulations Evidence-Based?

In my opinion, this is a very interesting point because psychology is a science and formulations are where the line between fact and opinion become blurred.

Evidence is 'a central process the role of scientist-practitioner' (Tarrier and Calan, 2003: 311)

The scientist-practitioner model is a widely accepted model of clinical practice by professionals.

You can read about this and other approaches to Clinical Practices in Clinical Psychology.

Furthermore, Deiling and Kuyken (2003) propose that a formulation should be able to survive a scientific investigation into its reliability as well as outcome.

Basically, we should be able to point to the evidence where the formulation came from.

Yet Bieling and Kuylen (2003) has demonstrated that the current evidence for formulation. At least the reliability in case formulation is modest at best.

But there's great paucity of research looking at the validity as well as the impact of case formulation on the therapy's outcome.

Showing that there is a small amount of evidence clearly showing the evidence of formulation in Cognitive Behavioural Therapy.

Although, there isn't a clear evidence base for individual case formulation.

Overall, there is no clear link between the evidence for formulation and its effectiveness in therapy.

Nonetheless, there's been no research into the validity

or where case formulation are related to the client's problem. (Kuyken et al, 2009)

Therefore, it's difficult to see how the therapy can ever proceed with a hypothesis about the client being there.

Additionally, it's odd how all the to-date research around availing, validity as well as the reliability seems to be judged by the therapist.

This is odd because doesn't the client matter?

Should it be up to them to decide if the therapy is valid or reliable?

Or shouldn't they at least have a say in the matter?

Additionally, this raises the questions of how could validity be measured in therapies or even the question of could it be measured at all?

If you want to know more about these issues, I recommend these two research papers:

- Barber and Critish-Christoph (1993)
- Messer (1991)

CHAPTER 26: TRUTH VS USEFULNESS

Formulation is 'the linchpin that holds theory and practice together' (Bulter, 1998: 1)

Continuing with our look at the debates surrounding formulation, I have to note that formulations are involved in a debate known as the Truth vs Usefulness.

This debates questions whether formulations are 'true' or just opinions, and if there's a tradeoff between a formulation's truth and its usefulness.

As a result, formulations are a therapist's hypothesis about the client's difficulties.

In other words, formulations are basically theories that can never be correct or true.

They can only be falsified. Messer (1996) and Bulter (1992: 21)

The Truth about the Truth

This has been my argument and something that I love to bring up in arguments because the idea of truth is so subjective.

For example, my truth about my actions might/ will be different to what you perceive as the truth about my actions.

Overall, there is no such thing as one version of the truth due to the different ways we construct our realities.

In other words, there are multiple versions of the same truth.

Additionally, individuals and families have different truths or understandings about the same conflict or situation.

For instance, if the mother of the family had an affair. Then the husband or wife might perceive the truth as the mother not caring about the family and being selfish.

Whereas the mother's truth might be the partner has been neglecting her for some time.

This makes it hard to see how formulation could ever be true or correct.

Unless we consider for a moment that some models

of therapy are 'truer' than others.

Interestingly, Bulter suggests that a formulation does not have to be true. It only has to be useful.

Personally, I love this idea because to me the job of a therapist is to better the lives of our clients. Meaning we need to produce useful formulations that can help improve and better the lives of our clients. By helping them to reduce or cope with their difficulties and alleviate the psychological distress they experience.

Meaning if we cannot achieve 'truth' but we can produce a formulation that is useful to the client, betters their lives and does NOT harm the client. Then I don't see the problem with that.

However, the concept of usefulness is subjective, so this makes it difficult to know if the formulation is useful.

On the other hand, Bulter resolved this problem for us because she suggests that a useful formulation will be very useful and be good at clarifying and organising information.

Therefore, we can communicate this clearly to the client and it helps to have an internal supervisor to over the therapist to make sure that they are producing a useful formulation.

Bulter (1998) Ten Tests of Formulation:

According to Bulter (1998), for a formulation to be useful, it needs to answer these questions.

- Does the formulation make theoretical sense?
- Does it fit with the evidence?
- Does the formulation account for the precipitating, predisposing and prepulating factors?
- Do other people believe the formulation makes sense?
- Can it be used to make predictions?
- Can you work out how to test these predictions? Such as: intervention or reactions to therapies.
- Does the past history fit?
- Does the treatment that the formulation is based on progress as you theoretically excepted?
- Can it be used to identify future sources of difficulties or risk?
- Are there important factors that are left unexplained?

CHAPTER 27: USEFUL TO WHOM

Useful for the client:

Hopefully, a formulation is always useful to the client, but people don't come to psychological services asking for a formulation.

Instead, clients come to us asking for help. To help them with their difficulties and mental health conditions.

To make this worse, there is a lack of, or research, into the views of client's on formulations.

The exception is to this is Chadwick et al (2003) that found 9 clients had found the formulation helpful to them understanding their problems.

Whereas 6 clients found the formulation reassuring and encouraging.

However, 6 people found the formulation to be saddening.

On the other hand, I would like to add that the 6 people who found the formulation saddening might have had a badly worded letter or the therapist's communication could be bad in these situations.

Regardless of if this is true or not, it's hard to draw long term effects from this single study.

Another potentially negative case study is Redhead (2010) who found some people found finding the cause(s) of their difficulties distressing.

To counter this, the rest of the studies and interviewed clients were positive.

Overall, I want to say that these two studies are not saying formulation is bad for clients because there is an awful lack of research on the topic. Making it impossible to draw real conclusions from them.

Finally, if you look at the studies above carefully then you'll see a lot more people like the formulations compare to those who don't.

Harmful to clients:

Like everything, when a formulation is done poorly, and the therapist doesn't follow the guidelines or principles laid out through this book. It can be harmful to clients.

For example, if a therapist ignores the client and/or doesn't co-construct the formulation with them. Then a number of outcomes could happen to the client and depending on the individual and the situation different outcomes could happen.

- The client could be traumatized by the service.
- The service could compound or maintain the difficulties.
- The client could dislike therapy and become resistant to change. Making the success of future interventions more difficult.

Another harmful feature of a formulation could be if the therapist ignores important information because it doesn't fit the model.

For example, if a therapist has a preference for Case Formulation in Cognitive Behavioural Therapy and the client is certain that their family is the source of the difficulties. Then the therapist may ignore this critical factor because it doesn't fit with the CBT model.

You shouldn't do this!

Useful to Therapist:

Thankfully, a formulation isn't only useful to the client because it can be useful to the therapist as well.

The main reason for this usefulness is because of validity, how the formulation applies to the real world. Due to a therapist feels better when a client endorses a formulation.

Also, a formulation can help to alleviate a therapist's uncertainty about the therapy as well as causes.

As supported by Yalom in Durmont (1993;203) who said our theories are self-created, wafer-thin barriers against the pain of uncertainty.

Personally, I quite like this idea because as a therapist you are in charge of a client's therapeutic success as well as you are meant to better their life.

This comes with massive responsibility and knowing that your decision could potentially make or break a client is a heavyweight on your shoulders.

Therefore, having something like a formulation to help relieve some of the uncertainty is very beneficial.

CHAPTER 28: INDIVIDUALISING NATURE OF FORMULATION

Formulation vs Diagnosis:

If you've read my book Clinical Psychology then you know that formulation isn't better than diagnosis because both processes are needed.

Personally, I prefer formulation but that's my own opinion.

As a result, diagnosis is needed to give the client a concrete description of their mental health condition, as well as the therapist needs the concrete that a diagnosis provides to give them a guide to a client's condition.

Finally, you need the individual-ness of formulation so the client can get the tailored intervention they need.

Are formulations individualising?

They can be individualising and whilst this can be great for the client. Due to it means the formulation is tailored to their own unique circumstances. It can be harmful if the therapist ignores personal and social contexts

Meaning this replaces the damage done by diagnosis.

Furthermore, another reason why individualising can be negative is because it can result in placing all the blame on the client. Making them the reason for all their difficulties.

I presume I don't need to explain why that's awful for a client?

Thankfully, the DCP Guidelines on formulation remind us all that clients are survivors of very difficult personal factors that are found at the individual level. As well as if we ignore that fact then therapists can make an already heighten sense of hopelessness even worse.

Key Question: Is Individualizing Inevitable?

In short, a formulation doesn't have to be individualising and there are attempts to change this by taking a systemic approach by looking at the difficulties in terms of the broader family.

In addition, to using community psychology so you

look at the client's problems through social action.

Psychologists like Ray Chowdhury (2003) have agreed that there are many ways to make individual psychotherapy not individualising. As well as there are many ways to integrate social as well as political factors into formulation

Finally, the DCP (2011:20) states 'critical awareness of the wider societal context within with formulating takes place even if the dimension is not explicitly included in every individual formulation;'

Can Anyone Construct A Formulation?

Unfortunately, the process or event of formulation isn't seen as essential by everyone, some see it as a waste of time and others don't even see it as a special skill.

As seeking to understand a client and their personal meaning isn't unique to the therapist as it is central to being human. Due to everyone wants to try and understand other people.

Building upon this further, as humans we formulate our own hypotheses about the social world and we test them. like a formulation.

This is key for psychological survival.

However, I love this next point because interestingly the people who hate and reject formulation still the same basic ideas!

So, they can't hate formulations that much!

For instance, Carl Rodgers rejected formulation but in his therapies and ideas, he emphasised the importance of being client-focused, finding the meaning of the client's experiences and focus on caution, sensitivity and being non-judgemental.

Weird, doesn't that sound a lot like formulation?

Self-Help?

Apparently, it is even argued that formulation can be used as a self-help technique.

Really!

As a result, some approaches and the humanistic approaches that reject the use of formulation. Still use techniques as well as strategies to help the client to reach some level of understanding about their psychological distress.

Basically, they still use formulation.

The key difference here is that in these other approaches here seems to be a greater emphasis on respecting the client's own views.

<u>Wrap Up:</u>

There's still one more chapter to go but I want to say that despite everything in this section, formulation is still great and useful.

So, don't let anyone tell you otherwise- as long as you're doing it correctly!

CHAPTER 29: CONCLUSION

Overall, as the final chapter in this book, I want to say thank you for joining me on this journey as we talk about formulation in psychotherapy.

Also, in this chapter, I wanted to summarise the most important points for you when it comes to formulation. Regardless of whether you are a current, soon to be or future therapist. You should find this chapter useful.

Consequently, to maximise the benefits of a formulation, regardless of the chosen model or approach, for everyone. Including the clients, services and teams. As well as minimize the negative effects of formulation. We need to:

- Use reflectivity
- Offer our formulation tentatively for both the teams as well as the individual.
- Construct all our formulation collaboratively with the client.

- Use a client's personal meaning as a central integrating factor.
- Always be open to re-formulating as new information comes to light.
- Communicate our formulation in normal, everyday language.
- Always consider the role of trauma as well as abuse.
- Always respect our team's and client's views on the usefulness as well as accuracy of the formulation.

Remember how I mentioned earlier in the book that my Clinical Psychologist lecturer pointed out that she was the clinical expertise, but the client is the expert in themselves.

- Ensure formulation are culturally sensitive.
- Be aware of stake-holder interests.
- Be willing to acknowledge the role of the service in compounding the effects of the client's difficulties.
- Always take wider socio-political as well as systemic factors into account.

If we want to take formulation into wider psychology and other disciplines to bring it into the mainstream. Then we need to:

- Be very cautious about entering conversations about a formulation's correctiveness or truthfulness.
- Carry out more as well as different types of research into the effects of formulation on the team, client, therapy, and therapists.
- Collect hard data on outcome measures. For example, admission, cost, staff morale and more...
- Completely abandoned the unsupported claims about the uniqueness of formulation to anyone- particularly professionals.
- Be willing to talk about the shortcomings of psychiatric diagnosis.
- Develop formulation-based alternatives for diagnosis as well as clustering as well as administrative tools.
- Be realistic yet confident about the use of formulation.

Now, you know a lot about formulation so please go out into the world and share this knowledge.

I truly believe formulation is a great and powerful tool that can potentially benefit everyone.

I hope you've enjoyed this book as much as I have loved writing it...

CONNOR WHITELEY

Bibliography:

Carr, A. (2012). Clinical Psychology: An Introduction. London: Routledge.

Davey G., Lake, N. and Whittington, A. (Eds). (2010). Clinical Psychology (2nd Edn). London: Routledge.

Beutler, L., Machado, P., & Neufeld, S. (1994). Therapist variables. In S. Garfield & A. Bergin (Eds.), *Handbook of psychotherapy and behaviour change* (4th ed.). New York: Wiley.

Crits-Christoph, P., & Stirman, S. W. (2011). Re: New Psychotherapies for Mood and Anxiety Disorders: Necessary Innovation or Waste of Resources?. *The Canadian Journal of Psychiatry*, *56*(4), 251-252.

Decker, S. E., Nich, C., Carroll, K. M., & Martino, S. (2014). Development of the therapist empathy scale. *Behavioural and cognitive psychotherapy*, *42*(3), 339-354.

Luthans, F. (2005). *Organizational Behavior* (10th ed.). Boston: McGraw-Hill.

Schroder, T. A., & Davis, J. D. (2004). Therapists' experience of difficulty in practice. *Psychotherapy Research, 14*(3), 328-345.

Eells, T. D. (1997). Psychotherapy case formulation: History and current status. In T. D. Eells (Ed.), *Handbook of psychotherapy case formulation*. (p. 1–25).

Gilbert, P. (2009). Introducing compassion-focused therapy. *Advances in Psychiatric Treatment*, 15(3), 199– 208.

Harper, D. & Moss, D. (2003). A different kind of chemistry? Reformulating 'formulation'. *Clinical Psychology, 25*, 6-10. ISSN: 1473-8279.

Johnstone, L (2013). Using formulation in teams. In L. Johnstone & R. Dallos (Eds.), *Formulation in psychology and psychotherapy: Making sense of people's problems* (2nd ed., pp. 216-242). London: Routledge.

Johnstone, L. (2018) Psychological Formulation as an Alternative to Psychiatric Diagnosis, *Journal of Humanistic Psychology*. 58(1), pp. 30-46.

Johnstone, L., & Dallos, R. (2013). *Formulation in psychology and psychotherapy: Making sense of people's problems*. London: Routledge.

Kuyken, W., Padesky, C. A., & Dudley, R.

(2008). *Collaborative case conceptualization: Working effectively with clients in cognitive-behavioural therapy.* New York: Guilford Press.

Tarrier, N., & Johnson, J. (Eds.). (2015). *Case formulation in cognitive behaviour therapy: The treatment of challenging and complex cases.* London: Routledge.

Walker, L. E. (1979) *The Battered Woman.* New York: Harper and Row.

Weatherhead, S. (Ed) (2015). Special Issue: Team formulation. *Clinical Psychology Forum, 275.*

Whiteley, C (2020) Abnormal Psychology 2nd Edition, CGD Publishing

Whiteley, C (2020) Clinical Psychology, CGD Publishing

Thank you for reading.

I hoped you enjoyed it.

If you want a FREE book and keep up to date about new books and project. Then please sign up for my newsletter at www.connorwhiteley.net/

Have a great day.

About the author:

Hello, I'm Connor Whiteley, I am an 18-year-old who loves to write creatively, and I wrote my Brownsea trilogy when I was 14 years old after I went to Brownsea Island on a scout camp. At the camp, I started to think about how all the broken tiles and pottery got there and somehow a trilogy got created.

Moreover, I love writing fantasy and sci-fi novels because you're only limited by your imagination.

In addition, I'm was an Explorer Scout and I love camping, sailing and other outdoor activities as well as cooking.

Furthermore, I do quite a bit of charity work as well. For example: in early 2018 I was a part of a youth panel which was involved in creating a report with research to try and get government funding for organised youth groups and through this panel. I was invited to Prince Charles' 70th birthday party and how some of us got in the royal photograph.

Finally, I am going to university and I hope to get my doctorate in clinical psychology in a few years.

Please follow me on:

Website: www.connorwhiteley.net

Twitter: @scifiwhiteley

Please leave on honest review as this helps with the discoverability of the book and I truly appreciate it.

Thank you for reading. I hope you've enjoyed it.

All books in 'An Introductory Series':

BIOLOGICAL PSYCHOLOGY 2ND EDITION

COGNITIVE PSYCHOLOGY 2ND EDITION

SOCIOCULTURAL PSYCHOLOGY- 2ND EDITION

ABNORMAL PSYCHOLOGY 2ND EDITION

PSYCHOLOGY OF HUMAN RELATIONSHIPS- 2ND EDITION

DEVELOPMENTAL PSYCHOLOGY 2ND EDITION

HEALTH PSYCHOLOGY

RESEARCH IN PSYCHOLOGY

A GUIDE TO MENTAL HEALTH AND TREATMENT AROUND THE WORLD- A GLOBAL LOOK AT DEPRESSION

FORENSIC PSYCHOLOGY

CLINICAL PSYCHOLOGY

CONNOR WHITELEY

FORMULATION IN PSYCHOTHERAPY

Other books by Connor Whiteley:

THE ANGEL OF RETURN

THE ANGEL OF FREEDOM

GARRO: GALAXY'S END

GARRO: RISE OF THE ORDER

GARRO: END TIMES

GARRO: SHORT STORIES

GARRO: COLLECTION

GARRO: HERESY

GARRO: FAITHLESS

GARRO: DESTROYER OF WORLDS

GARRO: COLLECTIONS BOOK 4-6

WINTER'S COMING

WINTER'S HUNT

WINTER'S REVENGE

Companion guides:

BIOLOGICAL PSYCHOLOGY 2ND
EDITION WORKBOOK

COGNITIVE PSYCHOLOGY 2ND
EDITION WORKBOOK

SOCIOCULTURAL PSYCHOLOGY 2ND
EDITION WORKBOOK

ABNORMAL PSYCHOLOGY 2ND
EDITION WORKBOOK

PSYCHOLOGY OF HUMAN
RELATIONSHIPS 2ND EDITION
WORKBOOK

HEALTH PSYCHOLOGY WORKBOOK

FORENSIC PSYCHOLOGY WORKBOOK

Audiobooks by Connor Whiteley:

BIOLOGICAL PSYCHOLOGY

COGNITIVE PSYCHOLOGY

SOCIOCULTURAL PSYCHOLOGY

ABNORMAL PSYCHOLOGY

PSYCHOLOGY OF HUMAN
RELATIONSHIPS

HEALTH PSYCHOLOGY

DEVELOPMENTAL PSYCHOLOGY

RESEARCH IN PSYCHOLOGY

FORENSIC PSYCHOLOGY

GARRO: GALAXY'S END

GARRO: RISE OF THE ORDER

GARRO: SHORT STORIES

GARRO: END TIMES

GARRO: COLLECTION

GARRO: HERESY

GARRO: FAITHLESS

GARRO: DESTROYER OF WORLDS

GARRO: COLLECTION BOOKS 4-6

GARRO: COLLECTION BOOKS 1-6

Business books:

TIME MANAGEMENT: A GUIDE FOR STUDENTS AND WORKERS

LEADERSHIP: WHAT MAKES A GOOD LEADER? A GUIDE FOR STUDENTS AND WORKERS.

BUSINESS SKILLS: HOW TO SURVIVE THE BUSINESS WORLD? A GUIDE FOR STUDENTS, EMPLOYEES AND EMPLOYERS.

BUSINESS COLLECTION

GET YOUR FREE BOOK AT
WWW.CONNORWHITELEY.NET

Printed in Great Britain
by Amazon

79287950R00102